# Crowdfunding –

# The next big thing?

How crowdfunding is evaluated by
different expert groups as a future model
of financing new ventures in Germany.

# Table of content

# 1   Introduction

The difficulties for entrepreneurs of getting financed are well known. They sometimes have huge problems to raise money in a very early state of their project. Own money is often missing, especially in case of young entrepreneurs after having finished university. Asking friends and families is not an option for every founder and bank loans are not always easy to get. For start-up teams who have already produced some kind of prototype or have received the first revenues, Business Angels or Venture Capitalists (VCs) are possible options. However, if start-up teams look for funding up to 200.000 Euro, crowdfunding is a new solution and will be the heart of this thesis.

Crowdfunding is an alternative way to raise money by attracting a crowd[1] of investors willing to spend small amounts of cash in exchange of equity, in

---

[1] The crowd is a huge audience, where each individual person will offer a small amount of money.

exchange for the product or just for donation reasons (Kleemann, Voß & Rieder, 2008). Crowdfunding can support different ideas and projects. Politicians, artists, and entrepreneurs have used it over the last years, even though the crowdfunding market is very young (Schwienbacher & Larralde, 2010). In this thesis the focus will be on founders of new ventures, who want to use crowdfunding as a financing method for their start-up. Entrepreneurs can use this new solution to finance their creative ideas and for marketing and small scale market testing (Kuppuswamy & Bayus, 2013). It seems to be a perfect option for new entrepreneurs. First researcher and especially the press got interested in this topic, too. *Süddeutsche Zeitung, Manager Magazin,* or *VC Magazin* are only a selection of German media, which published huge articles about crowdfunding in recent time.

But perhaps crowdfunding is only that interesting at the moment, because it is not largely used yet. The resource 'crowd' could be limited in future. Legal restrictions may follow and shut down the whole crowdfunding market in Germany. What do experts think of these issues? What is the opinion of entrepreneurs to use crowdfunding as a financing method? What do Venture Capitalists say, who spend lots of effort into evaluating business plans of new ventures? How does the press or scientists evaluate the trend of crowdfunding? Is it the future of funding a start-up or just a trend?

In this thesis these questions should by answered and it should provide a deeper understanding of the term and the process of crowdfunding as a financing method and give an estimation for its future by experts in this field.

It will start with the theory part in chapter 2. A financial overview of different methods to fund a start-up is followed by the explanation of the term of crowdsourcing, the overall concept of tapping a crowd. Crowdfunding in its three specifications, donation, pre-order and profit sharing (crowdinvesting), will be explained afterwards, together with the description of the process of a project. The chapters, portraying the chances and risks for the founders, the success factors and the motivation by the donators, are following. This leads to the description of possible future trends and the research question, where chapter 2 will end.

Expert interviews provide a variety of opinions on the topic of crowdfunding as a financing method for start-ups. The description of this method and the selection of the experts and the guide lining questions are presented in chapter 3.

The part presenting the results (chapter 4) will start with a summary of all concordant statements of the experts and is followed by the controversy opinions in an overview. Then the research questions are tested and further results of the interviews are demonstrated. Finally all interviews are summarized and presented before entering the discussion part (chapter 5). The different estimations by the experts in relation to the theory will be presented here. At the end of chapter 5, a summary of the recommendations for start-ups will be presented in a table, followed by a final conclusion of the thesis.

## 2 Theory

This part will introduce the reader to the terms and conditions of crowdfunding in its different specifications. At the moment the topic "crowdfunding" is all over the press and recently some scientific abstracts already got published. The leading papers with empirical analyses are from the authors Lambert & Schwienbacher (2010) and Belleflame, Lambert & Schwienbacher (2012). Belleflamme et al. (2012) analysed why ventures decided to use the crowdfunding as a pre-order model or crowdinvesting as a profit-sharing model. For them crowdinvesting makes sense when a larger amount of money is needed. Kappel (2009) differentiates between "ex ante crowdfunding" as the normal model of crowdfunding and "ex post facto crowdfunding" as a model, where the project is already finished. Schwienbacher & Larralde (2010) also published a paper about "crowdfunding of small entrepreneurials ventures" with a good overview of this topic in general.

In the following theory chapters, crowdfunding will be described as a financing method for start–ups discussing the chances and risks for entrepreneurs. Afterwards the description of the drivers to participation from the crowd and possible future trends will lead to the research questions.

## 2.1 Financial overview of starting a company

Before diving deeper into financing a start-up via crowdfunding, the traditional financing methods should be presented. New ventures have several options to raise money at the beginning. Own capital, loan programs and money from friends and family are the cheapest way to start a business. Bank loans, business angels and investors are more difficult to convince and more expensive, because you either have to pay a high interest rate or you have to give up shares. In either way your freedom to operate is limited, because capital providers want to know what happens with their money.

More recently, there is another option for entrepreneurs to finance their start-up called crowdfunding. Entrepreneurs directly seek money from the crowd via the Internet by presenting their projects (Kleemann et. al, 2008). A short overview of the traditional financing methods is shown in the chart below. The question whether or not crowdfunding will be integrated or will even replace one method is the main subject in this thesis.

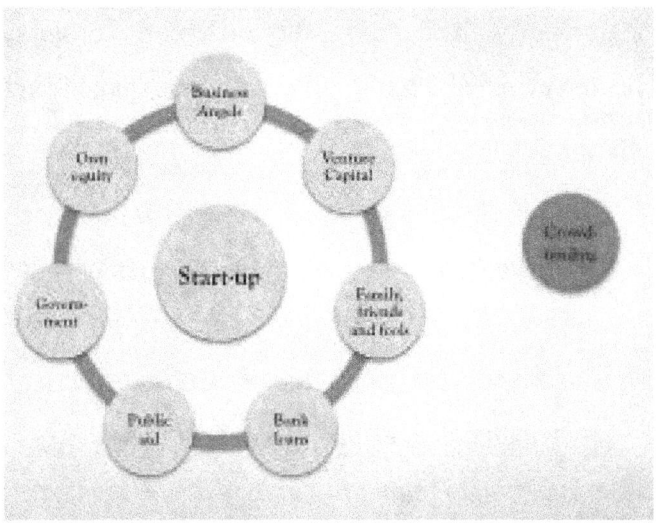

Fig. 1 Overview: Traditional financial methods and crowdfunding as new method, own source

## 2.2 Crowdsourcing

In 2006 the term crowdsourcing was first used by Howe: „The new pool of cheap labour: everyday people using their spare cycles to create content, solve problems, even do corporate R & D" (Jeff Howe, 2006). This quote reveals a lot about the term meaning that we do not need to outsource cheap labour to countries where the salary is low, but simply need to make use of the crowd via Internet for free.

Beginning with defining the different wordings, Kleemann et. al (2008) give an often quoted and very precise definition:

> *"Crowdsourcing takes place when a profit oriented firm outsources specific tasks essential for the making or sale of its product to the general public (the crowd) in the form of an open call over the internet, with the intention of animating individuals to make a [voluntary] contribution to the firm's production process for free or for significantly less than that contribution is worth to the firm"* (Kleemann et al., 2008, p. 6).

In conclusion crowdsourcing means that companies try to reach the crowd via Internet to receive feedback and new ideas to develop their business.

Crowdsourcing can be seen as the overall concept of different concepts using the crowd (Belleflamme et. al, 2012b). Howe (2008) defines four different concepts of crowdsourcing with the sub categories of crowd wisdom, crowd creation, crowd voting and crowdfunding.

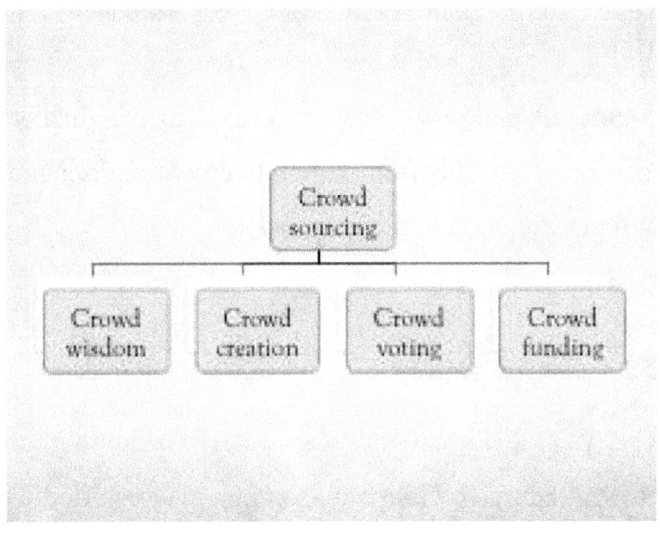

Fig. 2 The four concepts of crowdsourcing according to Howe (2008), own source

Platforms like wikipedia.com have also proven that crowds can be used differently. Here the crowd is not only social and creative, but the huge potential of information distributed by the crowd can be seen (Warner, 2012). In the early days of the Internet, the crowd was already used for fundraising. For their US tour the rock band Marillion from England raised $60.000 in 1997. Since this time the band used this financing model for records and marketing. There are lots of similar examples, especially of music or cultural background, where companies/bands etc. use the crowd to pre-finance their projects. This form goes into crowdfunding and will be explained in the next chapter.

## 2.3  Crowdfunding

The year 2011 can be seen as the beginning of crowdfunding in Germany. Entrepreneurs started to tap the crowd to directly seek financial help to start a new venture (Schwienbacher & Larralde, 2010). "The basic idea of crowdfunding is for an entrepreneur to raise external finance from a large audience (the "crowd"), where each individual provides a very small amount, instead of soliciting a small group of sophisticated investors" (Belleflamme et. al., 2012b). Crowdfunding is used as an open call via Internet to receive financial help. Three forms of crowdfunding can be identified: Donation-based, reward-based and profit-sharing (Kleemann et al., 2008).

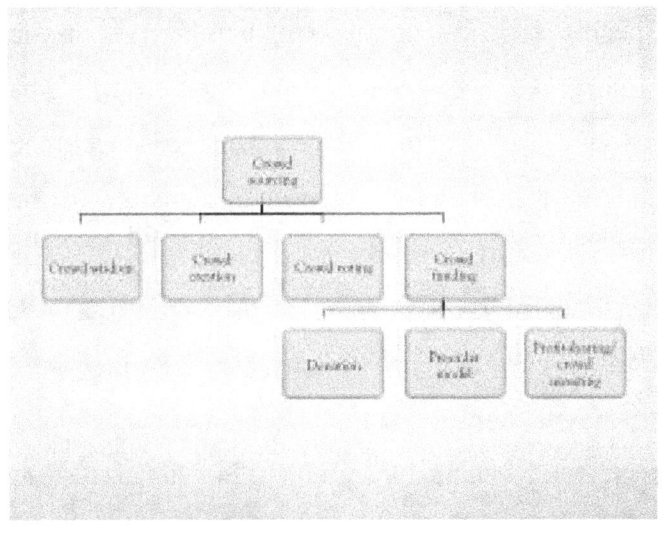

Fig. 3 The three concepts of crowdfunding according to Howe (2008) and Kleemann et. al (2008), own source

There are different reasons why companies decide to use crowdfunding as financing model. The main goal is raising money, but crowdfunding also helps enterprises in "testing, promoting and marketing their products, in gaining a better knowledge of their consumers' tastes, or in creating new products or services altogether" (Belleflamme et. al, 2012b). Furthermore compared to other financing methods crowdfunding is cost and time efficient (Kleemann et. al, 2008).

Specific products or projects, like film or music projects can be funded via the crowd. The individuals of the crowd get a cheaper product in the end for their financial support: a signature of the artist, a t-shirt or similar products. This concept is the so-called "ex post facto crowdsourcing" (Kappel, 2009). Schwienbacher & Larralde (2010) explain, "in simple terms, crowdfunding is the financing of a project or a venture by a group of individuals instead of professional parties (like, for instance, banks, venture capitalist or business angels)."

For different kinds of projects, there are different platforms. These crowdfunding websites are "a new form of social media that facilitate transfers of money to enable larger projects to find the funding they need" (Wash, 2013). According to the crowdfunding Monitor 2013[2], the following data collection of the End of 2010 until September 2013 can be summarized:

- 1.350 successfully financed projects, out of 2.758, → 49% success rate
- 5,80 Mio Euro collected money (in average 4.300 Euro per project)
- 153.134 Euro was the highest amount of a single project
- 19% got more money that planned (from 2012 to 2013)

The main German platform providers are shown in the chart below, categorized in different fields. Seedmatch.de and startnext.de are the main platform providers, when talking about funding entrepreneurs. But indigogo.de from the US is already entering the German market.

---

[2] More data is available at: http://www.fuer-gruender.de/fileadmin/mediapool/Unsere_Studien/Crowd_Q1_2013/Crowd_funding-Monitor_Q1_2013.pdf

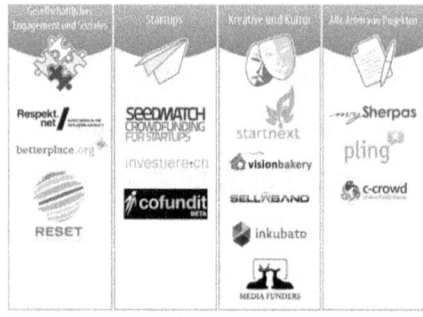

Fig. 4 German speaking crowdfunding platforms[3]

## 2.3.1 The process of crowdfunding a project

1. <u>Preparation phase:</u> First of all the funders have to set a minimum amount of money they need to start their project. This could start with 100 Euro, but could also go up to 100.000 Euro. Second, the founders have to set a timeframe in which they want to raise the money. This could be at least 60 days. Before producing a video, the founders have to decide what kind of incentives they want to offer to the crowd. In the cultural sector e.g. t-shirts from the movie or CDs with signature from the band are given as little presents, when a specific amount of money is donated.

---

[3] taken from www.smava.de

These presents are very important in order to get more money from the crowd than the minimum needed. You can pay 15 Euros for a nice CD in a pre-order model, but if the artist signs the CD, you probably pay 20 Euros. Some people will pay 50 Euros if they get invited to a band party or even 100 Euro if they get a backstage pass or a meeting with the band.

In preparation of the project, the founders have to describe their project and produce a video of it (see kickstarter.de), because the donators want to know to whom they give their money. This so called "pitch-video[4]" can also be seen as a good exercise to present the product/project in pictures and only a few words (Warner, 2012). The text version should be more precise and should include a business plan with some financial figures. This is very important for start-ups who want to do crowdinvesting, but not so essential for companies who are looking for crowdfunding, where the donation idea is in the focus.

---

[4] Advices for the pitch-video are collected in „The crowdfunding bible" (Steinberg, 2012)

2. Crowdfunding phase: Now, the crowd is invited to donate, to pre-order the product or to invest in the company (Belleflame et al., 2012). Mostly the product is now cheaper than it will be later to give an incentive for the first consumers. The funders talk to their network and encourage them to support their project. They collect fans, get the first feedback and try to reach as much funders as possible via their social media network (see startnext.de).

3. Finished project: If the amount of money, the founders set at the beginning of the project, is not reached by the end of the time that is given, all the money goes back to the donators. If the project is successful, the founder gets the money directly (minus a provision for the provider). This is called the threshold pledge system. It is no problem if they reach more than they wanted in the beginning. The donation widget then shows the percentage of how much they are over the set number. The donators can always see how much the project already reached and how successful it is. After a project is finished the donators can follow the development of the project via the provider platform.

To have the process of a crowdfunding project in an overview, the main steps in the different phases are described in the chart below:

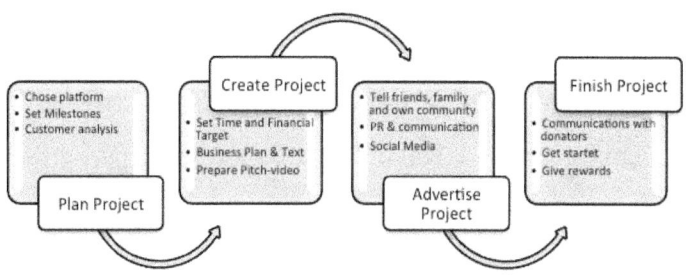

Fig. 5 Different steps in a crowdfunding process, own source

## 2.3.2 Crowdinvesting

Crowdinvesing is a special form of crowdfunding, where investors give money and get a share of the profits or equity in return (Belleflamme et. al, 2012b).

In 2012 there were 45 successfully finished projects in the field of crowdinvesting. 88 start-ups were funded till 30th September 2013. In total a sum of

8,3 Mio Euro was collected and the forecast for 2013 is a volume of 13-15 Mio Euro (Crowdfunding Monitor, 2013). In some countries the amount of investors a company may have is limited, therefore new ventures like to offer goods in exchange for money (Schwienbacher & Larralde, 2010). The typical sum of a successfully finished project is about 50.000 € - 100.000 € and therefore appropriate for seed financing. As we can see in figure 5 not only the overall funded amount of money has increased over the last two years, but also the number of platform providers has got bigger. Seedmatch.de, Companisto.de and Innovestment.de are not only the pioneers in the German crowdfunding market, but they have been also the platform providers with the most successfully finished projects until now (October, 2013).

A good overview with all German crowdinvesting platforms in comparison with legal issues, funding time etc. can be seen on deutsche-startups.de.

## 2.4    Chances and risks for start-ups

The main reasons why entrepreneurs choose crowdfunding for financing their start up are the financial support, the public attention and the feedback (Belleflamme et al. 2012b).

Crowdfunding can also be used as a means of market research. The founder team can see directly if the "crowd" pre-orders the product and what they say about it. It is a good opportunity to get quick and cheap first market testing. If the crowd likes the idea and the video, they will want to help the team to get funded. Now these new fans promote the project within their own community (Warner, 2012). Immediately people talk about the project. This form of viral marketing even before the official project is finished can be seen as another main reason why to choose crowdfunding as a financing method.

In comparison to the traditional financing models, crowdfunding has decreasing transaction costs, because of the use of online platforms. The platform providers take at least 10% of the funded sum, but this percentage pay the funders and not the founders.

If a start-up has already finished a project on a crowdfunding platform successfully, for some business angels or investors this is seen as "proof-of-concept" and the chances increase for a second financing round.

Starting a project on a crowdfunding platform can lead to new customers, but also to new partners for the business. The founders get new data from people who are interested in their project and the supporter can reach the founders directly via mail.

After some communication (rights, contracts, etc.) between the founders and the platform providers the pitch-video can go online. There is no long testing of the financial situation and the business plan via the bank or investors. After all, the founders remain the voting rights when they got funded. This enables them to react freely and their scope of actions remains undisturbed.

Whether or not the entrepreneurs tried to get money from a VC, with crowdfunding it is not only one person who judges the idea and the business plan, but hundreds of people. Even though most of the people are no finance experts, the chances are higher that some like the idea and donate. The independency from one VC can be seen as another advantage.

The average distance between the founders and the VCs is about 112km but the average distance between the founders and the supporters are about 5.000 km (Agrawal, Catalini & Goldfarb, 2011). Therefore via Internet you can reach a lot more supporters than via the direct offline way.

But there are also some disadvantages to go online with a project on a crowdfunding platform. Crowdfunding is not appropriate for every project. Especially in the B2B it does not seem to be easy, because the crowd named final-consumer is missing. It is important to stay in contact with ones investors, because they support the founders. However this direct contact via e-mail or phone can be time consuming and the pressure might cause stress. Staying within the time issue, most founders underestimate the time they need for the realisation of a crowdfunding project (Warner, 2012).

The funding sum is limited in Germany to 100.000 Euro. For some start-ups this is not enough and a second financing round is necessary. It is not always easier to start the next financing round, it can also become more difficult: The new investors or VCs do not want to have trouble with the number of the other smaller investors, or the contracts are too difficult up to that point (exit, etc.).

This thesis will not go into depth of the legal issues crowdinvesting will be facing in the near future. Also the complex and difficult contracts can be seen as disadvantages. For instance, exit-conditions and similar clauses can create problems, because of the big number of small investors.

Whenever people explain their idea at such an early stage, they run the risk, that others steal the idea and try to realize it faster or better. Not reaching their aim is also hard for the founders. This can cause negative marketing and might have a negative impact on the further search for investors or VCs.

Germans might be excited about crowdfunding, what they are not excited about is donating via paypal or credit card and so there have been some problems with payment of crowdfunding in the last months (Warner, 2012).

In the end "smart" money is missing. Business Angels or VCs could help when the start-up struggles at the beginning. The expert network and the professional advice are missing.

In the table below the main pros and cons of using crowdfunding for financing a start-up are presented in short form.

| Advantages | Disadvantages |
| --- | --- |
| Financial support | Payment methods |
| Public attention | Many small investors |
| Feedback | Legal issues |
| Market testing | Difficult contracts |
| Marketing | Stealing of idea |
| Low transaction costs | Difficulties for $2^{nd}$ round |

| | |
|---|---|
| Stepping stone for further investment | Bad marketing if failure |
| New contacts | No "smart" money |
| Quick access to money | |
| Remaining voting rights | |
| No dependency of one VC | |

Tab.: 1 Advantages and disadvantages of crowdfunding, own source

## 2.5 Success factors

Crowdfunding as a financing method is very new and thus there are no holistic academic studies on the success factors of crowdfunding. But some papers include basic ideas why some projects have been successful:

First of all, the entrepreneurs should have an interesting and innovative project, so that people get interested in the whole development of the start-up (Schwienbacher & Larralde, 2010). Secondly the total amount of money the entrepreneurs would like to get should be „reasonably low" (Schwienbacher & Larralde, 2010). In fact, there are laws in Germany, which restrict the level of money (see 2.3.1). Thirdly the entrepreneurs should have a look on other projects on the platform. Ward & Ramachandran (2010) state that people who donate have a closer look on other similar projects and their success rate. The crowd uses this information when they make their decision and donation. Therefore an orientation on other projects would make sense.

An important role in the final success of a project plays the social information (level of support, timing) of a project (Kuppuswamy & Bayus, 2013). Entrepreneurs should be aware of the fact that the crowd is not only donating because they like the idea or the entrepreneurs, but also because of the other funders (compare 2.6). Furthermore it is useful for the success of a cord funding campaign that the media reports on the project (Warner, 2012). To please the media and to entertain the crowd, it is useful to come up with a good story (Werle, 2013).

The entrepreneurs should be open-minded. People like to participate in crowdfunding projects, amongst others, because they like to be useful and help. Thus they should be interested in the opinion of their donator (Schwienbacher & Larralde, 2010)

The bigger the crowd and the better their network is, the higher are the chances to be successful. The "distribution channel Internet enables a maximum of range with minimal expenses" (Warner, 2012, p.3).

Finally, the chances of non-profit organizations to reach their capital target are very high (Belleflamme et. all, 2012a)

## 2.6 Motivation by the crowd

But why people take financially part in crowdfunding projects and what outcome they expect is the question in this chapter. It seems to be obvious that people who take part in crowdinvesting, are interested in profit. If we take a closer look at the typical crowdfunding investors, we see a 39-year old man with finance or innovation management background who already had first experience in the capital market (Hornuf & Klöhn, 2013).

**Sympathy**

Researchers from the University of Toronto tested the phenomenon „crowd" in the music business in 2009 and identified that the influence of friends and family in the early stage is very important and that this group represents 20% of the project budget (Agrawal et. al, 2011). Lawton & Marom (2011) are of the same opinion when they say, that most of the users support projects with a social relationship. These users are also very important at the beginning, because other donators see them as a proof of trust for the project and because they are the first who give money (Lawtom & Marom, 2011). Thus, sympathy and a strong emotional content are main drivers in the participation of a crowdfunding project (Giudici et.all, 2012).

## Involvement

No matter if we talk about crowdinvesting or crowdfunding, in any case, the customer is closely involved in the whole process. Whether the "crowd" acts as a customer or as an investor, they are involved in the company from the beginning and have an impact in the decision-making process of these firms (Belleflamme et al., 2012b). Being part of it from the beginning and helping others to achieve their goals (Gerber et al., 2012) are other drivers to participate in crowdfunding projects.

## Self-Expression

"We are what we post!" is the title of the paper of Schau & Gilly (2003) where they describe their study of self-expression via personal web space, where consumers use digital stimuli and hyperlinking to express themselves. Participating in a crowdfunding project and posting about it on Facebook or similar social media platforms shapes the own online identity in a specific direction. If crowdfunding gets more popular, the posts of people who show their funding affinities will increase (Lawton & Marom, 2010). Consequently this form of self-expression can be seen as social value for crowdfunding projects.

## Social Acceptance

A study showed that investors care about their social acceptance and that therefore non-profit companies are the most successful ones in the area of crowdfunding (Lampert et. al., 2010). Wang & Fersenmaier (2003) also state that status is one of the main drivers in the participation of a crowdfunding project.

## Future Consumers

Especially with pre-order projects on crowdfunding platforms, the supporting crowd will be the future users of the product or the service. Belleflamme et al. (2012b) show that „crowd funders donate because they expect to be consumers". Most of the time these future customers get a limited or special edition of the product. This lead-user mentality of being the first customer of the product is another driver to participate in crowdfunding projects.

**Community**

People prefer to take part in projects, when others seem to do the same (Klandermans & Tarro, 1988). Important is the all-or-nothing principle. The founders only get the money, when the amount of money they initially set is reached. Supporters who really want that the project will be successful will tell and motivate their friends to make it realise.

**Entertainment**

Last but not least it is always a risk to invest in start-ups, but most of the people simply enjoy supporting these new ventures. They like the start-up communities and are entertained when they observe their "baby" and see how it grows. This fun-factor is more important than other things like for example monetary incentives (Füller et.al, 2006).

There is a wide range of reasons why donators like to support the entrepreneurs. It is not only money or reward based, but more because of social reason like sympathy, connection with people and social networks (Gerber et al., 2012). Giudici et al. (2012) state that people are willing to invest, if the project has an emotional impact on the supporters, the donated money is low enough to deal with a loss and that the returns, which are only shared among the other investors, create an exclusive non-monetary benefit. A study of the New York Times (2012) shows that the crowd likes to support movies and music projects, but the highest amount of money with an average of $29.000 are reached in the area of design, games and technology.

There has been some research especially on the motivation of participation yet (Harms, 2007; Weng & Fesenmaier, 2003; Gerber et. al 2012) but there is still plenty of room for further research about the motivational aspects of crowdfunding. Depending on the form of investing i.e. donating or pre-order models, depending on the type of projects and lastly depending on the kind of marketing of the platform provider, there seem to be different motives to take part. These must be identified in the future, because it is indispensible for the success of a project to know what the consumer's motives are.

As mentioned before, there are many motives for involvement. These purposes can be divided in three categories: emotional, social and personal reasons. According to the current literature, the table below presents the main drivers of participation in crowdfunding projects:

| Why take people part in crowdfunding projects? | |
| --- | --- |
| Emotional reasons: | • Sympathy with idea or entrepreneurs |
| | • Emotional impact of project |

| | |
|---|---|
| | • Involvement in the development process |
| | • Helping others to archive their goals |
| Social reasons: | • Connection with people |
| | • Community thinking |
| | • Social acceptance; being part |
| | • Self-expression via social media |
| Personal reasons: | • High support of movies, music, design, games and technology |
| | • Amount of donated money is low |
| | • Future consumers |
| | • Entertainment |

Fig. 6 Motivation of donators, own source

## 2.7 Future trends

The potential of crowdfunding might not be tapped yet. In Germany only a few people know about crowdfunding at all. This lack of knowledge can cause an immense increase of the popularity of crowdfunding, if the subject becomes generally known. As presented in the chart below, there have been 1.350 projects and the amount of money, which has been collected, has increased to 5,8 Mio Euro in till 30th September 2013 in Germany.

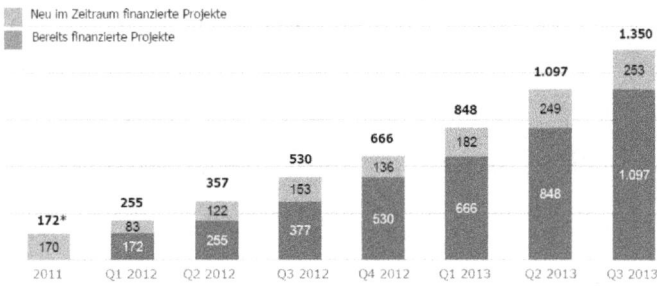

Fig. 7 Total number of financed crowdfunding projects[5]

## 2.7.1 Reaching the peak - Gartner's Hype Cycle

The success factors of crowdfunding are the absence of money for entrepreneurs, because of the on-going

---

[5] taken from: http://www.fuer-gruender.de/

financial crisis, the easy access to crowdfunding platforms via Internet and the success of the crowdsourcing (Agrawal et. al. 2011). These factors together seem to predict an increase of crowdfunding over the next months or years. The Gartner Hype Cycle also declared that crowdsourcing is on the upgrade. The expectations for crowdsourcing are increasing (see chart below). Currently crowdsourcing is in the technology trigger, but on the way to the top within the next five to ten years. Crowdsourcing is the overall concept of different crowd concepts, while crowdfunding and crowdinvesting are not differentiated. Therefore it is difficult to make a realistic preview on crowdfunding in terms of donation and pre-order models.

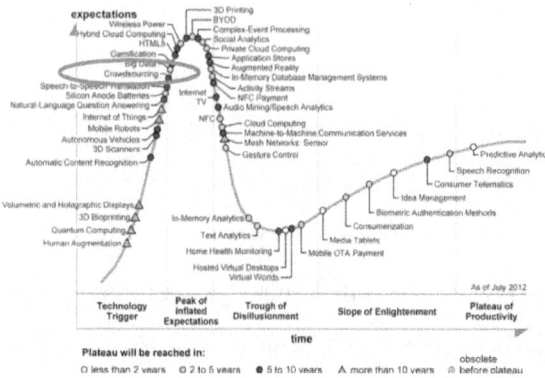

Fig. 8 Gartner Hype Circle for Technology 2012[6]

## 2.7.2 Problems with crowdinvesting

Even though crowdinvesting is an increasing market it still has "only" a volume of 6,5 Mio Euro in Germany (Hornunf & Klöhn, 2013). Above that Hornuf predicted in his presentation at the *Crowdinvesting symposium 2013* at LMU Munich that more companies will become insolvent, because more platforms will offer projects which won´t be extremely profitable. About half a year ago, the first platforms had to frequently announce failures of projects (see chart below). The red bars represent the number of not successfully finished projects up until

---

[6] taken from: clouduser.de

the time the founders set from Oct 2011 until Jan 2013.

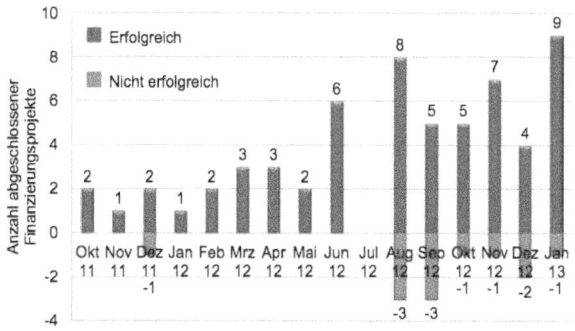

Fig. 9 Success and failure of projects on crowdinvesting platforms[7]

### 2.7.3 Upward trend of crowdfunding

Crowdinvesting seems to face problems in the closer future, because of legal issues in Germany. But crowdfunding may play "an important role at the very start of an entrepreneurial project´s life-cycle" (Giudici et. al, 2012).

With an increase of 160% crowdfunding projects that have been finished in 2012 compared to the year before (see fig.10), there have been 494 successfully finished projects and over 1,95 Mio € have been

---

[7] taken from: LMU Forschungsdatenbank

spend, which is an increase of 320% in relation to 2011. The Crowdfunding Monitor (2013) predicts that 5-6 Mio Euro will be collected in 2013, which will be a growths of 150% compared to 2012.

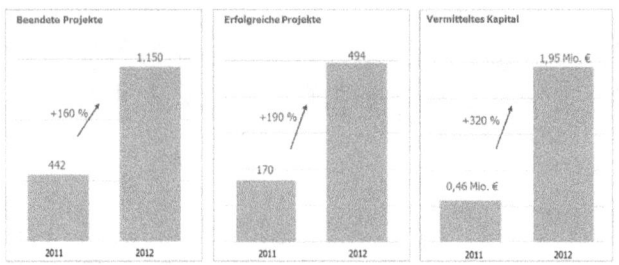

Fig. 10 Growth of crowdfunding 2011/2012[8]


## 2.8 Research questions

Crowdfunding is not only interesting for entrepreneurs who want to raise money, but also for the "crowd", people who are attracted by this phenomenon and for future investors. Being an entrepreneur is exciting and crowdfunding seems to be a fantastic option of financing a new venture. Therefore the following question occurs:

---

[8] taken from: http://www.fuer-gruender.de

**Start-up + Crowdfunding = The next Big Thing?**

Firstly, referring to the list of advantages for entrepreneurs, crowdfunding seems to be a great opportunity for start-ups, whereas the disadvantages are less significant until now (compare 2.4). Secondly, not only the press, but also more and more scientific papers proof the increasing importance of crowdfunding as such. The conferences in Berlin (April, 2013), the symposium (March, 2013) and the Dialog Conference (November, 2013) in Munich are other signs that the popularity of crowdfunding rises in Germany. The increase of the amount of collected money from 2,4 Mio Euro at the End of 2012 up to 5,8 Mio Euro at the end of September 2013 (Crowdfunding Monitor, 2013) indicates further grows. Therefore the first research question can be made:

**Research question 1:**

*The trend of crowdfunding will increase in the future in Germany.*

Referring to the Crowdfunding Monitor (2013) the increase of 320% of the funded capital from 2011 to

2012, the idea of using crowdfunding to start a company enjoys great popularity. But the fact that in Q3 2013 over 200% of the volume of the funded money of 2012 was already reached demonstrates huge success. If this growth continues, which is also shown by the Gartner Hype Circle, crowdfunding might replace other financing methods in future. Therefore the second research question follows:

**Research question 2:**

*Crowdfunding will replace traditional financing methods like VCs for start-ups.*

As stated by Giudici et. al (2012) crowdfunding is probably not able to replace VCs , but may be another financing method for start-ups. Keeping in mind that crowdfunding faces some big problems like the missing "smart" money and network. The problem of second financing rounds as well as that it might be only appropriate for specific projects lead to the third research question.

**Research question 3:** *Crowdfunding will be an alternative to the existing traditional financing models.*

# 3    Method

## 3.1    Expert interviews as qualitative research method

This research is based on expert interviews in the field of crowdfunding in Germany. First of all, the reason why expert interviews make sense in this research is that crowdfunding is not yet very well known in the general public. Therefore a qualitative research method with e.g. a large number of questionnaires would be very difficult to accomplish. Secondly, talking about crowdfunding means talking about money. This is a sensitive topic and means to act with caution. Thus it is best to talk directly to people. Thirdly, complex questions can be discussed in detail and the interviewer can ask for more detailed information to get a better understanding of the statements. Consequently the depth of data grows, which is the biggest advantage. One of the main disadvantages of this qualitative research is the big expenditure of time in comparison to quantitative methods (Bortz & Döring, 2002).

## 3.2 Selection of the expert groups

To get representative results different expert groups should be interviewed. First of all, the expert must be defined. The question of who is an expert can only be answered by the research questions (Mey und Mruck, 2010). In this research all experts have to have a thorough knowledge of financing new ventures with crowdfunding as one funding method. While the research questions are all around the topic of crowdfunding as a financing model for start-ups, the experts should ideally either have build up a company on their own or work with entrepreneurs on a daily basis.

Good interview partners are a key driver of the successful performance of the research method and should be selected carefully. For the selected interview partner the following questions according to Jäger & Reinecke (2009) have been very helpful: Who has relevant information? Who can give precise information? Who will give information? Which experts are available? After an intensive search for appropriate candidates the following experts have not only a huge knowledge but were also willing to take part in the interview. Finally the number grew up to eleven interview partners, which are briefly described now.

### 3.2.1 Platform providers

It seems to be obvious that platform providers know a lot about crowdfunding, because they are leading a company in this area. There are three experts from this group as interview partners. The most successful and "oldest" platforms in the area of crowdfunding and crowdinvesting in Germany are seedmatch.de and innovestment.de. The company mash-up finance started in 2012 and is not only located in Munich, but also focussing the support of Bavarian start-ups.

**Jens-Uwe Sauer, seedmatch.de**

The founder of the famous platform seedmatch.de, Jens-Uwe Sauer, is an interview partner in this research. He used to work as a consultant for entrepreneurs with a focus on funding new ventures before he founded seedmatch.de in August 2011.

**Thomas Herzog, innovestment.de**

Thomas Herzog, founder of the second biggest platform innovestment.de is an expert in the interview in March 2013. He has been one of the speakers at the *Crowdinvesting symposium 2013* at LMU Munich.

**Dr. Levin Brunner, mashup-finance.de**

Dr. Levin Brunner, founder of mash-up finance is the third interview partner in the group of platform providers. He is very active in the start-up scene in Munich and can be called one of the experts.

### 3.2.2 Entrepreneurs

The next experts, whose opinions are of interest, are the entrepreneurs, who thought a lot about financing a start-up. Every expert of the following group already knows a lot about crowdfunding and their opinions about it differ at lot. It is interesting to interview a founder, who successfully finished a crowdfunding project. On the other side, it is important to also have an opinion of a founder, who is against crowdfunding for financing new ventures.

### Dr. Björn Anton, mibaby.de

Dr. Björn Anton started his new venture with a successfully funded project. He raised 100.000 Euro in November 2012 for miBaby via seedmatch.de and talks about his impression of crowdfunding in this interview.

### Catharina van Delden, innosabi.de

Catharina van Delden, entrepreneur and founder of innosabi comes from a crowdsourcing background and can be seen as expert in this branch. Innosabi helps companies to integrate customers in the innovation process.

**Elisa Birr, myroomstyle.de**

Elisa Birr, founder of MyRoomStyle, decided not to use crowdfunding to finance her start-up. She comes from a financial background and occasionally still works as a consultant to finance her own start-up.

### 3.2.3 Opponents

The third expert groups are the opponents, people who work in the area of financing start-ups and know a lot about funding. There are many different ways how entrepreneurs can finance their new venture (see 1.1), and VCs is one of them. Research question two is about replacing other financing methods like VCs. Therefore it is important to interview this group of opponents. The following interview partners are from different companies with very different expertise.

**Tim Diesel, Mountain Spring AG**

Tim Diesel is currently a VC at Mountain Spring AG, a global investment holding. He founded his own company in 2009 with financial support from VCs and the government program *EXIST* for entrepreneurs.

**Dr. Carsten Rudolph, evobis GmbH**

Dr. Carsten Rudolph is CEO of evobis GmbH and head of the official Munich business plan competition. He is well connected with business angels and investors in Bavaria and always supports start-ups with his network and know-how.

**Andreas Unseld, UnternehmerTUM-Fonds**

Andeas Unseld is the investment manager of the UnternehmerTUM-Fonds. He and his team finance start-ups, which mostly come from the TU Munich. Their focus is on early stage financing.

### 3.2.4 Other experts

To round the selection of experts it is interesting to have an interview partner with scientific background. As already known, there are not many papers published yet about crowdfunding. However one professor, who is an expert in the field of crowdsourcing was willing to answer the questions. After reading a lot about crowdfunding, it becomes clear, that most of the articles are written by only a few journalists. One of them is also an expert in this research.

### Prof. Dr. Frank Piller, RWTH Aachen University

Prof. Dr. Frank Piller is chair professor of management at the Technology & Innovation Management Group of RWTH Aachen University. Frank Piller´s research focuses on co-creation of the company´s value with the inclusion of the customers.

**René S. Klein, journalist**

René S. Klein is journalist at fuer-gruender.de. He published a number of articles about crowdfunding and designs many interesting info graphics about the whole subject. Who ever gets in touch with crowdfunding will know his media work.

After the selection and inquiry process, eleven experts took part in this research, although the initial number of people who were asked to take part had been bigger. Mostly entrepreneurs were not willing to participate. The main reason was the lack of time; especially after they had successfully finished a crowdfunding project.

The selection of eleven people, with a variety of backgrounds as described above, have not only a very specific knowledge in the field of crowdfunding, but are also willing to talk about their experience and estimations. They allowed using their full name to support the credibility for this research.

### 3.3    Interview Guideline

After a short introduction the interviewees are asked to talk about crowdfunding as a financing model for start-ups. Therefore the following developed guiding questions should be answered:

1) What is your opinion on crowdfunding?
2) According to the current numbers, crowdfunding seems to be the future of financing a start up. What is your opinion on that?
3) How could the future of financing a start-up look like?

As an entry to this topic, a general question on crowdfunding will be the start. *"The trend of crowdfunding will increase in the future in Germany"* is the first research question and it can be answered with question number two. It is important to ask why-questions here to get a deeper insight into the interviewee's point of view on the future of crowdfunding. *"The role of the traditional financing methods will be replaced by crowdfunding"* is the second research question and could be answered with the third introductory question of how the future of financing a start-up could look like. This question is also the starting point to get more backed information about the future role of crowdfunding. By seeking deeper into the concept of the future of financing, research question three can be answered: *Crowdfunding will be an alternative to the existing traditional financing models.*

## 3.4  Implementation

Every interview differed from the other. Most of the interviews have been face-to-face interviews, some of them where telephone interviews. The average time of an interview was about one hour. Two people decided to answer the questions via mail, because of time and distance reason. In the first mail they answered the open questions and in a second mail they answered the follow-up questions. The interviews were transcribed directly afterwards to avoid understanding mistakes.

# 4 Results

In this chapter the most important results of the expert interviews are presented. The summary of the answers is approximately one page to make them comparable and is attached in the appendix. After the concordant statements, the opposed statements are documented. Finally, to present a good overview for the discussion, every interview is recapped to 4-5 rows with the most important statements of the interview.

## 4.1 Concordant Statements

Some statements came up in almost every interview. The experts know a lot about the topic crowdfunding and sometimes they agree on the same issues. In the short table below, these assertions are summarized.

| Crowdfunding... |
| --- |

... is not new!

... is not good for every kind of project!

... has many advantages like:

- Marketing via attention through social media

- Market testing

- Innovative way of getting investors

... can attract business angels for further financing!

... might have a positive impact on the increase of more start-ups!

... will be another financing method for start-ups!

... might be interesting also for big companies!

Tab.: 2 Agreements on issues of crowdfunding

## 4.2 Statements in comparison

As seen above there are some statements about crowdfunding which all experts share. But there are also opinions, where they differ a lot. The next tables show diverse opinions in the confrontation according to the research questions.

| The role of the VCs in future | |
|---|---|
| Thomas Herzog, INNOVEST AG | Tim Diesel, Mountain Partners AG |
| "The VC model will be overcome by a model where it is cheap to finance. There is no need of a VC anymore, when you can get financing first and then produce." | "I, as a VC, don´t have the impression that crowdfunding threatens our branch. Crowdfunding never had an impact on our daily business. Venture Capitalist Investors will always play a big role!" |

| The role of the incubators in future | |
|---|---|
| Tim Diesel, Mountain Angels AG | Dr. Levin Brunner, mashup-finance |
| "I am convinced that | "Incubators are difficult, |

funding start-ups via the company building of the incubators will increase." | because they only provide co-working and infrastructure and mostly not the required money to start a company"

## The role of crowdfunding in the future (I)

| Jens-Uwe Sauer, Seedmatch | René S. Klein, journalist |
| --- | --- |
| "In the next three years, crowdfunding will be an established possibility of financing new ventures." | "I doubt that we will reach circumstances like kickstarter in the US." |

## The role of crowdfunding in the future (II)

| Thomas Herzog, INNOVEST AG | Prof. Dr. Frank Piller, scientist |
| --- | --- |
| "Crowdfunding will be a major part of the | "There will always be the usual form of |

financing landscape for
start-ups!"

financing!"

| The right stage to use crowdfunding | |
| --- | --- |
| Jens-Uwe Sauer, Seedmatch | Tim Diesel, Mountain Partners AG |
| "Crowdfunding is interesting in every stage, also when competitors like VCs, banks and business angel show up!" | "Making the idea public in a stadium where they have not launched yet, seems not to be a good possibility for every start-up." |

| Network and contacts | |
| --- | --- |
| Jens-Uwe Sauer, Seedmatch | Catharina van Delden, Innosabi |
| "The founders team increase their network with crowdfunding and | "Traditional ways of funding provide contacts and networks, that |

| gets lots of supporters." | crowdfunding cannot offer (yet) to a similar extend." |

| Reaching the peak | |
| --- | --- |
| Jens-Uwe Sauer, Seedmatch | Dr. Levin Brunner, mashup-finance |
| "But we think: The full potential is not tapped yet! We feel the demand of the investors who ask us again and again, if there is another share here or there!" | "In my opinion the zenith is already reached. We are at the top of the hype circle of crowdfunding and crowdinvesting." |

## 4.3  Testing the research questions

Even though it is difficult to answer the research questions with a clear yes or no, most of the statements were definitely leading in one direction.

The overall opinions of the experts with a pure yes-/no-answer as a result from the whole interview are summarized in the three charts below. "Yes" means that the expert agree with the research question and "no" means disagreement.

**Research question 1:**

| The trend of crowdfunding will increase in the future in Germany. | | |
|---|---|---|
| Jens-Uwe Sauer | Seedmatch | yes |
| Thomas Herzog | Innovestment | yes |
| Dr. Levin Brunn | Mash-up Finance | yes |
| Dr. Björn Anton | miBaby | yes |
| Catharina van Delden | Innosabi | no |
| Elisa Birr | MyRoomStyle | no |
| Anreas Unseld | UnternehmerTUM-Fonds | no |

| | | |
|---|---|---|
| Tim Diesel | Mountain Spring | no |
| Dr. Carsten Rud | Evobis | no |
| Prof. Dr. Frank ] | RWTH Aachen University | yes |
| René S. Klein | Fuer-gruender.de | no |

Tab.: 3 Outcome research question 1, own source

Although expert interviews are part of qualitative research, by counting the yes/no answers the distribution seems to be balanced. The experts with positive experiences with crowdfunding like all platform providers (they earn money with this) and Prof. Piller see an increase in the trend of crowdfunding. The six other experts cannot see a constant growth.

**Research question 2:**

| Crowdfunding will replace traditional financing methods like VCs for start-ups. | | |
|---|---|---|
| Jens-Uwe Sauer | Seedmatch | no |
| Thomas Herzog | Innovestment | yes |
| Dr. Levin Brunr | Mash-up Finance | no |
| Dr. Björn Antor | miBaby | no |
| Catharina van Delden | Innosabi | no |
| Elisa Birr | MyRoomStyle | no |
| Anreas Unseld | UnternehmerTUM-Fonds | no |
| Tim Diesel | Mountain Spring | no |
| Dr. Carsten Rud | Evobis | no |
| Prof. Dr. Frank | RWTH Aachen University | no |
| René S. Klein | Fuer-gruender.de | no |

Tab.: 4 Outcome research question 2, own source

Thomas Herzog is the only one who confirms the distinct research question that crowdfunding will substitute other financing methods. He is convinced that VCs won´t be needed anymore. All other experts cannot see crowdfunding as big as VCs in the future of financing start-ups. The word "replace" might be a little too strong in this context.

**Research question 3**

| Crowdfunding will be an alternative to the existing traditional financing models. | | |
|---|---|---|
| Jens-Uwe Sauer | Seedmatch | yes |
| Thomas Herzog | Innovestment | yes |
| Dr. Levin Brunn | Mash-up Finance | yes |
| Dr. Björn Anton | miBaby | yes |
| Catharina van Delden | Innosabi | yes |
| Elisa Birr | MyRoomStyle | yes |

| | | |
|---|---|---|
| Anreas Unseld | UnternehmerTUM-Fonds | yes |
| Tim Diesel | Mountain Spring | yes |
| Dr. Carsten Rud | Evobis | yes |
| Prof. Dr. Frank ] | RWTH Aachen University | yes |
| René S. Klein | Fuer-gruender.de | yes |

Tab.: 5 Outcome research question 3, own source

This research question is proven without any dissentient vote. Even though some have more trust and other have some doubts, all experts see crowdfunding as one possibility to finance start-ups in the future.

## 4.4 Further results

All experts knew the difference between crowdfunding as a donation and pre-order model and crowdinvesting. Even though the experts where never asked to say something about crowdinvesting, in every single interview this was one issue they talked about. Not even one question focussed on the future problematic of crowdinvesting, but they all expressed their opinion about the legal issues in the close future during the interview. For them this topic seems to be very important and in close context when talking about crowdfunding.

## 4.5    Summaries Single Results

As last topic in this chapter, all interviews are summarized in 4-6 lines to see the similarities and differences at one glance and to give an overview before entering the discussion part. As usual the order is from platform providers to entrepreneurs, opponents and other experts in the last part.

**Jens-Uwe Sauer:** Jens-Uwe Sauer sees the future of financing a new venture via the crowd very positive, because the founders' team does not only get the money, which is needed, but also the attention via social media channels, where the investors are seen as multiplicators. Secondly the attention attracts business angels for further investments and thirdly the potential is not reached yet.

**Thomas Herzog:** Financing models like VC, where only a few people evaluate a new venture, will decrease and crowdfunding, where it is cheap to finance more businesses will increase. For Thomas Herzog this is a mega trend and instead of first producing and then selling, crowdfunding offers it the other way round.


**Dr. Levin Brunner:** As a platform provider Dr. Levin Brunner sees crowdinvesting facing some legal problems, but he is positive about crowdfunding. Also saying that it is not new, it will turn into a common financing method for start-ups after the "crash", which will be pretty soon. After recovering crowdinvesting will be systematic and transparent to the consumers.


**Dr. Björn Anton:** Dr. Björn Anton is, after raising 100.000 Euro, a big fan of seedmatch and finds the positive effects like getting a lot of new customers in a very early stage important and sustainable. Crowdfunding will not replace VCs, but simply be another possibility of raising money for start-ups at the beginning. Germans might like to give money to start-ups via these platforms, because they can reduce the risk of losing money, while spreading it over different projects.

**Katharina van Delden:** Katharina van Delden says that marketing and market testing, together with an innovative way of getting investors are the main advantages of crowdfunding. In her opinion traditional financing methods provide contacts, networks and expertise that crowdfunding nowadays cannot offer.

**Elisa Birr:** Preparation and marketing of the project are two disadvantages of crowdfunding at the beginning of a project for Elisa Birr. Competition and contracts with further investors are other problems just like the missing business network and experience of the business angels.

**Tim Diesel:** Tim Diesel sees crowdfunding not in competition with the traditional VCs, because "smart" money is missing. It never had an impact on the daily business of a VC, who will always play a big role. In future not only crowdfunding will be interesting for some start-ups, but also the financial support of the incubators will become more important.


**Dr. Carsten Rudolph:** Crowdinvesting is interesting, but problematic for Dr. Carsten Rudolph. Crowdinvesting could cause difficulties for follow-up investments, so crowdfunding seems to only be interesting for start-ups, which need little money. For Rudolph the number of business angels will increase as it did in the last few years.


**Andreas Unseld:** In his opinion, crowdfunding will only work, if the entrepreneurs need a small amount of money. The VC trend will decrease and more private individuals will invest more than 10.000 Euro. IT-start-ups will become more capital efficient and therefore the typical VC support will also decrease.

**Prof. Frank Piller:** Although Prof. Frank Piller thinks that crowdfunding is not new, it will be another financing channel in the future for start-ups. Especially in the time after the first prototype, crowdfunding can be a good possibility to finance a start-up, but it will also be used for marketing in the future.

**René S. Klein:** In future crowdfunding won´t be the only financing tool for start-ups, even though it is an alternative way to finance projects. But the crowd will become more selective and the start-ups also have to fulfil their promises to the crowd. First testing of ideas and market research are the obvious advantages of crowdfunding. New ventures will combine different financing models in the future and VCs might have to reconsider their role.

# 5 Discussion

In the following chapter the research questions will be discussed. Furthermore other future trends of financing a start-up will be presented. Finally a chart is shown at the end of this discussion part, which has been developed for entrepreneurs to check, whether crowdfunding could be suitable for their start-up.

## 5.1 The different future scenarios of crowdfunding

The first research question, if the trend of crowdfunding will increase in the future in Germany was answered very diversely. By knowing that more and more entrepreneurs think about crowdfunding as a financing method for their start-up, the idea itself clearly enjoys popularity. A 320% increase of the funded capital from 2011 to 2012 (see chapter 2.7) shows a straight upward trend for this funding method, but the opinions of the experts differ a lot.

### 5.1.1 The platform providers' point of view

Jens-Uwe Sauer and Thomas Herzog are very positive about the future of crowdfunding. Their platforms have been very successful until now and they also feel the hype through the media and the demand for interviews, as Herzog said in the interview. But even though they think about crowdfunding as a 'mega trend' they also know that crowdinvesting faces a big problem: legal issues. They know that the disaster is waiting to happen, but still, both act very positive about the future of their business.

Readers might think that Dr. Levin Brunner is a VC instead of a fully convinced platform provider for crowdfunding, because he is not as optimistic as his competitors are. He seems to be very realistic and not very euphoric. By knowing that he only does *mashup-finance* part-time and that his vision is to sustainably support start-ups in Munich, his personal financial interest stays in the background. In his opinion the potential of crowdfunding is tapped yet and it is only a question of time until the big crash of this new branch will come. Afterwards regulations, clear rules and transparent contracts are needed in his estimation. Brunner´s opinion is not concordant to the Gartner Hype Circle (see chapter 2.7.1) where crowdsourcing as such still has remaining time to reach the peak.

### 5.1.2 The opinion of the entrepreneurs

Dr. Björn Anton is very happy about the successful target he reached with *miBaby*. He is an absolute fan of crowdfunding and would use it as a financing method any time again. Catharina van Delden from *innosabi* is very interested in the whole topic of crowdsourcing, crowdfunding and crowdinvesting. She is also positive about the future of it and still sees an increase in the sector. Besides the role of the money aspect, for her the two additional benefits of marketing and market testing are the leading advantages for the entrepreneurs. Van Delden is of the opinion that there should be more platforms, which focus on different types of projects. Then not only the founders, but also the donators can choose the most appropriate platform.

As already seen by the diverse opinions of the platform providers, the entrepreneurs also do not agree in their estimation about the positive future trend of crowdfunding. Elisa Birr, *MyRoomStyle*, decided not to raise money via an online crowd. In the interview she said, that she would be afraid of steeling the founder´s ideas and that she does not want her business plan to be online. For her the disadvantages of crowdfunding outweigh the advantages. Coming from a finance background, she is also aware of the fact that contracts with crowd investors might cause problems with future investors. Therefore she is not optimistic about the future of crowdfunding and estimates this funding method as very difficult.

### 5.1.3 The estimation of the opponents

All three experts evaluate new ventures, business plans and founders teams and therefore have a deep knowledge of funding and supporting start-ups.

Whether it is the opinion of Diesel, Rudolph or Unseld, they all think that crowdfunding only makes sense for start-ups where only little money is needed. Unseld said that the costs for new ventures are very high (due diligence, management, etc.) and thus crowdfunding is a good opportunity for entrepreneurs who are not in the focus of traditional investors. Rudolph sees the start-ups with 'immediately useable consumer goods' have a good chance to raise money via the crowd.

But making the idea public in a very early stage and the deficiency of 'smart' money are two reasons why Diesel does not see the future of financing a start-up in crowdfunding. This topic never had impact on his daily business as a VC and therefore he doesn´t see it as a trend.

The follow-on investments might be very difficult for new ventures which were already funded by the crowd, said Rudolph in the interview. In his point of view the upcoming legal problems will have a negative impact on the whole crowdsourcing branch. For Rudolph another problem that crowdfunding will face in future is the cost of the platform providers. They do not earn enough money yet. And if they will earn more in the future, because they will have more successfully funded projects, competitors will appear and have a negative impact on their earnings. Therefore no investor will want to invest in crowdfunding platforms anymore, which is a huge problem for the provider.

### 5.1.4 Other opinions on crowdfunding

Another aspect Prof. Piller mentioned in the interview about crowdfunding is the pressure the entrepreneurs will have after they successfully raised money through a crowdfunding platform. The founders have to produce the product they already sold. Some of them have difficulties to stay within their timescale and will face problems with the customers waiting for the product. Piller thinks similar to the VCs and Birr that talking about the idea in such an early stage might attract competitors. He also considers that crowdfunding might be a good solution to finance the start-up during the time after the first prototype, but not during the development of the idea.

Journalist Klein estimates that crowdfunding will not reach circumstances like Kickstarter in the US. Crowdinvesting makes more sense than crowdfunding and is an easy way to gain access to financial means in his opinion. Klein knows a lot of advantages of crowdfunding, but also sees the chances for success not being realistic for every new venture. His estimation as a journalist for crowdfunding is very neutral.

## 5.2    The future of traditional financing methods

'Crowdfunding will replace traditional financing methods like VCs for start-ups' is the second research question. The wording 'replace' might be too strict in this context. Ten out of eleven experts see no replacement of traditional financing methods with crowdfunding. But the opinions still differ a lot, as we can see in the following section:

## 5.2.1 The role of the VCs

As it is demonstrated in section 4.2 where statements in comparison are shown in tables, the estimations of platform provider Herzog and the VC Diesel are very different. Herzog says that the VC model is very expensive and that crowdfunding has enormous advantages as a model where you first get financed and then produce. In contrast Diesel thinks that crowdfunding will not have any impact on the VC branch, because VCs are not interested in start-ups, where only little money is needed. As we can already see, research question two (crowdfunding will replace traditional financing methods like VCs for start-ups) can be discussed controversially.

The platform providers are convinced that crowdfunding will be very successful. If they did not have this opinion they would not have started a business in this field. For them the advantages of crowdfunding overweigh the disadvantages. For Sauer crowdfunding is interesting in every stage of financing. But the opposite opinion is represented by the VCs Diesel, Unseld and Rudolph, and also professor Piller. For them crowdfunding might be a good solution after the first prototype is produced and when only little money is needed in the beginning. Another reason why VCs might be replaced by crowdfunding is the huge increase of the network. For Sauer, the crowd is seen as multiplicator when posting and chatting about the project. For Herzog the VCs will face problems in the future, because of the overall VC model itself. Some smart guys select the 'right business' and the founders have a lot of effort and difficulties to please the few VCs.

Brunner thinks that some entrepreneurs tend to do crowdfunding, especially the ones who work with the lean start-up approach. Others prefer to get financed by VCs. For him VCs will have no competition from crowdfunding platforms in future. Van Delden is also convinced that the traditional ways of funding a company will not disappear, because these methods provide contacts and networks as well as management and market expertise. Crowdfunding can´t offer this yet. On this VC Diesel remarks that they can support the entrepreneurs with real help (with contracts e.g.) whereas the crowd wants to be entertained. Additionally the VCs have no time to search on all platforms to find good new ventures to finance in his point of view. However VCs like to see a 'proof-of-concept', says Diesel. A successful crowdfunding project and first revenues could increase the interest of VCs financing a new venture. Therefore the stadium of investing might change for the VCs, because of crowdfunding, so Diesel.

For the journalist Klein, crowdfunding can never be a substitute for VCs, but VCs might reconsider their role. Until now VCs had no real competitors, but this currently changes and the VCs should be aware of the new method of financing a start-up.

### 5.2.2 Business angels and private investors

Unseld sees, like the platform providers Herzog and Sauer, a decreasing trend for VCs being the financial supporters, but not because of crowdfunding. In his opinion more and more private investors will give more than 10.000 Euros and therefore the importance of VCs will be reduced. Also Rudolph thinks that there is a lot of scope for Business Angels. The investment range between 150.000 Euros up to 1 Mio Euro is not covered yet and there are many possibilities to fill this gap.

For Sauer business angels should help entrepreneurs after they have successfully raised money via crowdfunding. For him entrepreneurs can reach business angels easily with a crowdfunding project, because they observe the scene on these platforms. Additionally the entrepreneurs do not have to convince the business angels anymore after they have successfully finished a project and the business angels offer their financial support afterwards.

## 5.3   Crowdfunding - the next big thing?

Although crowdfunding is not interesting for every start-up, as Diesel or Rudolph say, all experts agree that it is a new solution of financing new ventures. This is not only because of the money, but moreover because of the advantages of testing, promotion and marketing as heard from Birr, van Delden or Pillar, but also already stated by Belleflamme et. al. (2012b).

Start-ups will be more able to combine different financing methods, says journalist Klein. In his opinion crowdfunding enriches the financing opportunities for start-ups and crowdfunding can be seen as another option of financing new ventures, which is the third research question.

The entrepreneur Anton thinks that crowdfunding will not be 'the' future, but a potential pillar. For the *miBaby* team it was also another possibility to generate customers, where Anton sees another advantage of crowdfunding besides money.

In summary the research question three that crowdfunding will be an alternative to the existing traditional financing models, can be answered positively. It is just the extend of the positive answers where the experts differ, but all experts are aware of the facts, that crowdfunding is another financing form for start-ups and therefore the figure in the theory chapter 2.1 can be extended with a new financing method: crowdfunding.

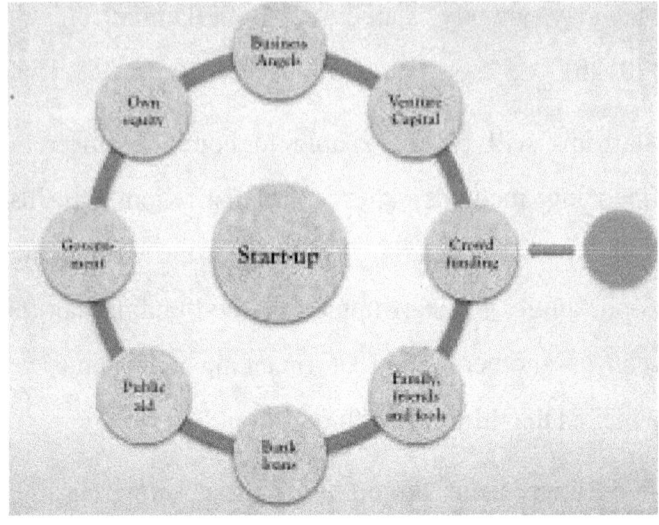

Fig. 11 Crowdfunding as another financing method, own source

## 5.4 Crowdinvesting and legal issues

Even though crowdinvesting was not the topic in the interview and none of the questions focussed on this, every one of the experts expressed their opinion on it. This proves that everybody is aware of the problems crowdinvesting will face in the future and that this issue seems to be very interesting for those involved in this sector. As well as the fully booked *Crowdinvesting symposium 2013* at LMU Munich a large number of press articles show that crowdinvesting is gaining popularity while facing huge problems with legal problems.

Each expert who has been consulted for this thesis knows about the risk of crowdinvesting and the upcoming legal problems in the future. Especially the VCs talked intensively about the legal issues crowdinvesting is facing. Tim Diesel sees it as 'a question of the German legislator in future' by knowing that after the 'crash' crowdinvesting will be simply another financing method.

## 5.5    More future trends

Most of the interviews were set within a timeframe of about one hour, so many other aspects arose during this time, which have not been mentioned yet. The most important thoughts of the experts in context with the future of crowdfunding are summarized below.

### 5.5.1 Thoughts about online start-ups

IT-Start-ups will be more capital efficient in future says Unseld of the UnternehmerTUM-Fonds. Therefore the average amount of money needed until break-even might be about 200.000 Euro. VCs are not interested to invest this amount of money, so the volume of VC projects in the online business might shrink. Entrepreneurs who want to produce an App might use crowdfunding as a pre-order model for financing during the time of development. Diesel sees crowdfunding for new ventures with a 'tangible technology background' as an interesting possibility to finance the start-ups at the beginning. For him government aid would not be the right financing form, because high class USPs like patents are usually required and mostly not owned. He is also convinced that successful internet company owners, who had a successful exit, open an incubator to support new founder teams during the idea-shaping. They will also finance the teams at the beginning.

### 5.5.2 More cultural decisions based in the crowd

The crowd can decide which start-up they want to support. They donate for a specific project or product. Whether they want to rebuild a playground in the city or to support a new classical music group, the weight of their voice on who they want to support in the cultural sector will get bigger. In the end official decision makers like politicians or authorities might have to include the crowd. Incorporation with the crowd especially in the cultural area is a good possibility to finance community projects with a social aspect in the future as the entrepreneur Birr sees the future of the overall crowdsourcing issue.

### 5.5.3 Uncertain future of platform providers

Another issue, which arose during the interview about the future of crowdfunding, is the financial part of the providers. Until now no platform is making profit (Zeit online, 2013). But how many successful projects does a platform need to get into the black? Dr. Levin Brunner was very clear about this problem to be coming up soon. By taking about 10% from a successful project until now platform providers can´t have break-even yet. Until now most of the platform providers have investors themselves. But who will invest in those platforms, if they are not profitable? And if the trend of crowdfunding will increase, more platforms will launch. This leads to more competition and the entrepreneurs can choose the platform for their projects. This might cause fewer projects even if the trend of crowdfunding will increase.

Last but not least, the US market leader kickstarter.de especially attracts German artists, because of the worldwide community this platform has and can be seen as a huge competitor for the German crowdfunding scene.

For Brunner, these are some reasons to only run the platform mashup-finance part-time and not to focus too much on profit, but more on local sustainability in Bavaria.

## 5.6    Recommendations for start-ups

Crowdfunding is a good option for artists, who need money to work on their projects in the music or film sector. But crowdfunding is also an option for start-ups. In the end the entrepreneurs have to decide whether they go for crowdfunding or not. A combination of the theory of crowdfunding and the expert interviews lead to some advice for start-ups, which consider using crowdfunding as a financing method. These most important requirements for start-ups are presented in the following table:

| Requirements for crowdfunding as the right financing option for start-ups | |
| --- | --- |
| Financial issues | • Only little money should be needed. |
| | • Start-up is not in the focus of investors. |
| | • Incentives should be selected carefully and should create a |

| | non-monetary benefit |
|---|---|
| Product issues | • It should be an interesting and innovative product/project. |
| | • Product/project should be strongly emotional |
| | • Consumer goods should be immediately useable. |
| | • The first prototype should have already been produced to show it to the crowd and to ask for money for further development or directly for production. |
| Customer issues | • Start-ups should focus on a B2C model. |
| | • Customers should have an immediate benefit from being one of the first to buy the product. |
| | • Customers in the close |

| | |
|---|---|
| | environment should like the idea, because family and friends are the first and therefore the most important donators at the beginning of a project. |
| | • The awareness of the press is important to attract more donators |
| | • A good story is important |
| Personal issues | • Entrepreneurs must have strong nerves, because the pressure to deliver afterwards, the communication with the donators and the keeping with the timescale will cause stress. |
| | • Good know-how in web 2.0 |

Tab.: 6 Requirements for start-ups

# 6 Conclusion

Crowfunding is a new financing method in the field of funding new ventures. Experts like the founder of seedmatch.de or innovestment.de, VCs and entrepreneurs agree that crowdfunding entered the German market as a funding method. This new way of financing can be the gap filler between bank loans and VCs and might attract more people to start a company in future, because it is time and money efficient.

Fig. 12 Crowdfunding in the financing model over time, own source

Crowdfunding will not replace other financing methods like VCs or business angels, but they are likely to be affected in terms of the scheduling of investment. Investors might invest at a later stage in average or use successful crowdfunding projects as a proof-of-concept for their evaluation.

All experts in this study see market testing and marketing as additional advantages of crowdfunding. Furthermore crowdfunding can be considered as virtual word-of-mouth propaganda while receiving feedback from the crowd. The founder´s team should be willing to take this response to develop the idea or to improve the prototype.

Entrepreneurs like the idea of pre-selling the products (Belleflamme et. al, 2012b). This could lead to a new form of business model where companies might not look for consumers, but for pro-sumers. Emotional and innovative projects, which only need a small amount of money to start with, have the best chances to reach the financial target. Therefore crowdfunding is a good option for entrepreneurs who focus on creativity or social issues instead of financial benefit. 96% of all entrepreneurs, who are already successfully funded, would use this financing method again (IKOSOM, 2011). This very large percentage shows the popularity of crowdfunding from the entrepreneur´s point of view and could be advertisement for future founders.

Further research in the field of motivation of the entrepreneurs to use crowdfunding is needed. More studies should also analyse the success rate of new ventures later on compared to start-ups using different financial methods. But not also the topic of crowdfunding in general deserves more research. Further surveys should focus on donators, founders, platform provider and opponents, especially with means of quantitative research methods. The more the crowdfunding community knows, the better they can influence a positive development. With a better understanding of the topic, new platforms can offer specific solutions within the industry-sector. Therefore further knowledge is needed.

Crowdfunding platforms are not cost-efficient yet. Some platform providers started to explore new business segments. Startnext.de builds new platforms for local providers like some German cities. Nordstarter.org for example is a creative crowdfunding platform for people in Hamburg.

This social thought of crowdfunding might increase in future, as we can already see that social projects are the most successful ones yet. A co-financing method, where foundations and the crowd support start-ups together might develop in the future.

There will arise more specifications on crowd-x, systems to use the crowd not only to get money or ideas, but also for decision-making. Democratisation of the economy or even for political issues may be possible future trends of crowdsourcing as an umbrella term.

In the end crowdfunding is not only an alternative financing method for start-ups with lots of advantages, but it also opens a new chapter of using the crowd for different issues.

# 7 List of references

Agrawal, A., Catalini C., & Goldfarb A., (2011). The Geography of Crowdfunding. NBER Working Paper, No. 16820.

Belleflamme, P., Lambert, T., & Schwienbacher, A. (2012). Individual Crowdfunding Practices. Available at SSRN 2151179.

Belleflamme, P., Lambert, T., Schwienbacher, A. (2012). Crowdfunding: Tapping the Right Crowd, in: CORE Discussion Paper No. 2011/32

Bortz, J. & Döring, N. (2002). Forschungsmethoden und Evaluation für Human- und Sozialwissenschaftler (3. Aufl.). Heidelberg: Springer Verlag.

Füller, J., Bartl, M., Ernst, H., & Mühlbacher, H. (2006). Community based innovation: How to integrate members of virtual communities into new product development. Electronic Commerce Research, 6(1), 57-73.

Gerber, E. M., Hui, J. S., & Kuo, P. (2012). Crowdfunding: Why people are motivated to post and fund projects on crowdfunding platforms.

Giudici, G., Nava, R., Lamastra C.R., & Verecondo, C., (2012) Crowdfunding: The New Frontier for Financing Entrepreneurship? Available at http://ssrn.com/abstract=2157429

Harms M., (2007) "What Drives Motivation to Participate Financially in a Crowdfunding Community?", Master Thesis Marketing, vrije Univerisiteit Amsterdam.

Hornuf, L. & Klöhn, L. (2013). Crowdinvesting und Portfoliodiversifizierung – Eine rechtsökonomische Anlayse. Venture Capital Magazin, 2/20013, 34-35

Howe, J. (2006). The rise of crowdsourcing. Wired magazine, 14(6), 1-4.

Jaeger, U., & Reinecke, S. (2009). Das Expertengespräch als zentrale Form einer qualitativen Befragung. Empirische Mastertechniken der Marketing-und

Managementforschung. Wiesbaden: Gabler Verlag, 29-76.

Kappel, T. (2009). "Ex ante crowdfunding and the recording industry: a model for the U.S.?," LLAE Law Review, 29, 375–385

Klandermans, B., & Tarrow, S. (1988). Mobilization into social movements: Synthesizing European and American approaches. International Social Movement Research, 1(1988), 1-38

Kleemann, F., Voß G. & Rieder K., (2008). Un(der)paid Innovators: The Commercial Utilization of Consumer Work through Crowdsourcing. Science, Technology & Innovation Studies 4, 5-26.

Kuppuswamy, V., & Bayus, B. L. (2013). Crowdfunding creative ideas: The dynamics of project backers in Kickstarter.

Lambert, T., & Schwienbacher, A. (2010). An empirical analysis of crowdfunding. Louvain–la–Neuve: Louvain School of Management, Catholic University of Louvain.

Lawton, K., and D. Marom (2010). The Crowdfunding Revolution. Social Networking Meets Venture Financing. Amazon Digital Services.

Mey, G., & Mruck, K. (Eds.). (2010). Handbuch qualitative Forschung in der Psychologie. Springer DE.

Rubinton, B. (2011). Crowdfunding: disintermediated investment banking. Available at SSRN 1807204.

Schau, H.J., Gilly, M.C. (2003), We are what we post? Self-presentation in personal web space, Journal of Consumer Research, 30, 385-404.

Schwienbacher A. & Larralde B. (2010). Handbook of Entrepreneurial Finance, Crowdfunding of Small Entrepreneurial Ventures. Oxford University Press

Steinberg, S. M., & DeMaria, R. (2012). The Crowdfunding Bible: How to Raise Money for Any Startup, Video Game Or Project. J. Kimmich (Ed.).

Wang, Y., & Fesenmaier, D. R. (2003). Assessing motivation of contribution in online communities: An empirical investigation of an online travel community. Electronic Markets, 13(1), 33-45.

Ward, C., & Ramachandran, V. (2010). Crowdfunding the next hit: Microfunding online experience goods. In Podcast retrieved from http://www. cs. umass. edu/~ wallach/workshops/nips2010css/papers/ward. pdf.

Warner, A. (2012) Krautfunding: Deutschland entdeckt die Dankeschön-Ökonomie, e-book, Amazon Distribution.

Wash, R. (2013). The value of completing crowdfunding projects. Working Paper.

Werle, K. (2013). Breit angelegt. Manager Magazin, 4(2013), 100-105.

## Online Sources

Deutsche Start-ups: 6 Crowdinvesting-Plattformen im Vergleich

http://www.deutsche-startups.de/wp-content/uploads/2013/01/Crowdfundingvergleich.pdf

13.04.2013

Fuer-gruender.de: Crowdfunding Monitor 2013

http://www.fuer-gruender.de/kapital/eigenkapital/crowd-investing/monitor/

01.02.2013, 19.04.2013, 22.04.2013, 08.11.2013

IKOSOM: Crowdfunding Studie 2010/2011

http://www.ikosom.de/2011/06/13/crowdfunding-studie-2011/

18.04.2013

LMU Forschungsdatenbank: Überblick über den deutschen Crowdinvesting-Markt http://www.uni-muenchen.de/forschung/service/wiss_transfer/gruenderbuero/download/hornuf_crowdinvestingsymposium.pdf

01.03.2013

New York Times: Three years of kickstarter projects.
http://www.nytimes.com/interactive/2012/04/30/technology/three-years-of-kickstarter-projects.html

21.03.2013

Süddeutsche Zeitung: Crowdfunding erwirtschaftet fast drei Milliarden Dollar

http://www.sueddeutsche.de/wirtschaft/projekt finanzierung-per-schwarm-crowdfunding-erwirtschaftet-fast-drei-milliarden-dollar-1.1644473 13.04.2013

Zeit online: Das leise Sterben der Crowdfunding-Plattformen

http://www.zeit.de/digital/internet/2012-08/crowdfunding-plattformen-deutschland

13.03.2013

# 8    Appendices

## 8.1    Platform providers

**Jens-Uwe Sauer, Seedmatch**

What is your opinion on crowdfunding?

Many people help with a small amount of money to reach a huge investment sum. Seedmatch offers this model to young ventures in the early stage. With this seedmatch started a change of paradigm in financing start-ups in Germany in 2011. It proves that crowdfunding works in Germany, with a (up to now) 100% success rate and funding dynamics of a few hours until the funding limit.

According to the current numbers, crowdfunding seems to be the future of financing a start up. What is your opinion on that?

We think that crowdfunding is not only interesting for seed financing, but also in every other stage where competitors like VCs, banks and business angels show up. We get more and more requests from start-ups who only want this form of financing. With crowdfunding the start-ups not only get money, but also a lot of supporters, which is not the case with typical financing forms. The founder teams increase their network. But the biggest advantage is the crowd: The investors will be multiplicators, if they post and chat about the new venture in social media platforms. With this talking about the new product, the increase attention and some start-ups get a huge competitive advantage, which they won´t get with other solutions of financing.

Business Angels help start-ups on top of the investment sum and are private investors. This is another reason to show how sustainable crowdfunding is and that crowdfunding positive a long time after the project has been on our platform.

How could the future of financing a start-up look like?

Until now we got over 3,3 Mio from the crowd, which is a huge amount of money. But we think: The full potential is not tapped yet. And also our investors ask again and again, if there is another share in this or that start-up, which is another proof, that of the huge potential. The demand is obvious. In the next three years, crowdfunding will be an established possibility of financing new ventures. This will be the next step of a bank free financing model. There will be a increase of professionalism of the industry. Furthermore we work on a legitimation of the branch or this kind of money investment in the public.

Thomas Herzog, INNOVEST AG

**What is your opinion on crowdfunding?**

Crowdfunding overall is a mega trend, which is based on the decreasing transaction costs realized by the use of online internet platforms with a fixed set of rules. It will be a regular part of financial transactions. In the long run it will eliminate some old fashioned intermediates - like the internet did already in a lot of other areas. Finance is known for not being innovative: the ATM was the only big innovation in banking (before online banking) for more than 50 years!

**According to the current numbers, crowdfunding seems to be the future of financing a start up. What is your opinion on that?**

It will be a major part of the financing landscape for start-ups. Overall the VC model - where some very smart guys try to select the right business - will be overcome by a model where it is cheap to finance a set of business and simply wait which one will florish – the ones that florish will get bigger amounts of cash. It will be much more evolutionary - what is a nice strategy to cope the inherent uncertainty.

How could the future of financing a start-up look like?

I pitch for getting cash for the prototype - afterwards I pitch for a Series A or alternatively simply do factoring in a way that I first sell and afterwards produce my product like it is done with the pebble[9] like products on kickstarter. There is no reason to have somebody like a VC to get financing to first produce and afterwards sell - I simply sell before production.

---

[9] The Pebble E-Paper Watch is a smartwatch developed by Pebble Technology. They launched a Kickstarter campaign on April 11, 2012, with an initial fundraising target of $100,000, but within two hours of going live, the project had met the $100,000 goal and within six days, the project raised over $4.7 million.

## Dr. Levin Brunner, Mashup Finance UG

**What is your opinion on crowdfunding?**

We finance start-ups, which want to grow organically with our crowdinvesting platform. Our investors focus on a long cooperation. With Web 2.0 this finance model began and is very new. But the idea of crowdfunding is older. Sellaband[10] started in 2006 with crowdfunding in the music business. You can see similar stories on ebay. How many sellers sold their products first, and then produced them?

**According to the current numbers, crowdfunding seems to be the future of financing a start up. What is your opinion on that?**

In my opinion the zenith is already reached. We are at the top of the hype circle of crowdfunding and crowdinvesting. I see the difficulties mostly in the area of crowdinvesting, because of the legal issues. Whenever a company will be bankrupt a thunderstorm will start. Layers will fight and the press will talk very negative about the whole usage of the crowd to start

---

[10] SellaBand is also a platform provider focused on musicians and supports artists with their next music project, funded by their fans.

business. But whenever that happens it regulates afterwards. And in the end it will even out in the middle. In the long run, I think that the thematic of first selling and then producing will be more transparent. Founders will tell the crowd that they have not started yet, but are willing to do so, if the customers are there. Founders with the lean-start-up approach might like to use crowdfunding more than others. But it will be in no concurrence to VCs.

How could the future of financing a start-up look like?

Crowd finance solutions will increase. But a strong standardisation will be important. The whole process must be systematic and more transparent, because until now, every platform provider has got different contracts, rules, etc. But for crowdfunding, I think, that this will be a financing model for start-ups to raise money quickly. Big companies will also use the crowd: They will integrate for example a developer and give them shares instead of money; same with other workers. In my opinion the typical work-for-money idea will turn into a work-for-being-part-of-it system. I am also thinking about incubators, but in the end, I do not see them in the future of financing start-ups, because they do not give them money, but only provide infrastructure or/and network and the contracts are horrible until now. But this might chance in future. I also thought about incubators. But incubators are difficult, because they only provide co-working and infrastructure and mostly not the required money to start a company.

## 8.2    Entrepreneurs

**Dr. Björn Anton**

What is your opinion on crowdfunding?

When we started to raise money for *miBaby*[11], we thought that crowdfunding is no solution for us. But in the end, we raised 100.000 Euro via seedmatch. This was not only very quick, but we also felt the positive effect of the crowd. Over 200 people pushed us; it was amazing.

According to the current numbers, crowdfunding seems to be the future of financing a start up. What is your opinion on that?

I think crowdfunding will not be "the" future, but a potential pillar. Crowdfunding will never displace the typical funding methods, like VCs. For us it was another possibility to generate customers, which is very important. This is a big advantage, because it is very sustainable to get the first real customers for

---

[11] An independent platform, which provides everything in the area of Babyshopping (see mibaby.de)

*miBaby.*

How could the future of financing a start-up look like?

I have no idea. I cannot predict the future, but until now crowdsourcing overall is very new and trendy and everybody talks about it. But like every trend the decrease will come sooner or later and afterwards it will settle down in the middle. We should not forget the Germans love to save money, and that there is a lot of money in our country. Instead of giving the money to one department, people might think of spreading their money to many options to decrease the risk of losing it. Crowdsourcing can be one possibility. People can give little money to more founder teams. And also our VCs are not really brave in Germany. Crowdfunding and crowdinvesting could gain momentum into the dusty VC scene. Last but not least, I think that there might be more founders in Germany, because they can test and rework their ideas and prototypes without a lot of effort[12].

---

[12] It took the founders of *miBaby* exactly two weeks to set up the project on seedmatch.

What is your opinion on crowdfunding?

Crowdfunding does not only provide an innovative way to approach investors, but offers two valuable additional benefits: Marketing, even before the product has been launched (often with hundreds of units sold before they are produced) and market testing (if people do get excited for an investment, they probably get excited as consumers as well). Those aspects are, in my opinion, most interesting, coming from a crowdsourcing background.

According to the current numbers, crowdfunding seems to be the future of financing a start up. What is your opinion on that?

If start-ups go for crowdfunding, they have to identify the most appropriate crowdfunding platform for their company – since, in terms of the future, of crowdfunding platforms I do see niche solutions as a necessary development.

How could the future of financing a start-up look like?

In my opinion, you have to ask them, which goals they

pursue with their investment strategy. I don´t think that "traditional" ways of funding a company will disappear – in providing contacts and network, as well as management and market expertise they often provide benefits, that crowdfunding can´t offer (yet) to a similar extend.

## Elisa Birr, MyRoomStyle GmbH

What is your opinion on crowdfunding?

In my opinion it is for some start-ups a great opportunity to raise capital. Especially for the seed phase it is difficult for start-ups to get funding in Germany. There are so many great business ideas out there that lack financing and sometimes even small amounts can have a major impact. And the marketing potential of crowdfunding is of course huge.

However, it needs a lot of preparation and marketing to get the necessary amount of people to vote for your start-up. Moreover, in a lot of cases the idea gets published before the current business starts and this might attract harmful competition. Sometimes the contracts with crowd investors are disadvantageous for future rounds. I think the main disadvantage is that you don´t get the business network and experience e.g. a business angel would bring along.

According to the current numbers, crowdfunding seems to be the future of financing a start up. What is your opinion on that?

I think there will be diverse forms of funding for start-ups. As mentioned above not all start-ups benefit from crowdfunding. E.g. for B2B start-ups crowdfunding will be very difficult to acquire. It will become very difficult to raise the necessary amount via crowdfunding once start-ups are in later stages.

How could the future of financing a start-up look like?

In my opinion the more different options for funding are out there, the better it is for start-ups. Private business angel and corporate funding should become as common in Germany as it is in the UK or the U.S. It probably will be a more global market in the future so that e.g. business angels from the U.S. fund more often European start-ups and vice versa.

## 8.3 Opponents

What is your opinion on crowdfunding?

Crowdfunding is a valid form of fundraising, but not interesting for every kind of start-up. Making the idea public in a stadium where they have not launched yet, seems not a to be a possibility for every start-up. Another disadvantage of crowdfunding is, that the money is not "smart", even though the donator/investor can contact the founders. Whereas angels or VCs can help with contacts, the crowd must almost be entertained. I, as a VC, had not the impression that crowdfunding threatens our branch. Crowdfunding never had an impact in our daily business. We also had no time to go to a crowdfunding platform and search in a mass of thousands ideas to identify the good ones.

But ideas who are not in the focus of traditional investors, crowdfunding is a great opportunity. But this is not true for every project.

According to the current numbers, crowdfunding

For crow investing this will be a question of the German legislator in future. Investors get equity stake for money, which is written in their contracts and notarially certified, which is not common in the US. For charity reason and donation the donator only needs a contribution receipt. Crowdfunding is mix form between both forms and a compensation for investments. Finally, I think, that there will a form of crowdfunding in future as a fix method of financing start-ups, and there will also always be stumbling blocks.

How could the future of financing a start-up look like?

Venture Capital Investors will always play a big role. But we can see a financing shift according to the stadium of development in start-ups. Investors like a prof-of-concept and an already successful launch. Investors are also happy to see an increase of revenues. Government aid won´t be success in the online world in the closer future, because they often require high class USPs like patents, which typical internet start-ups do not have in the beginning. But for new ventures with a "tangible" technology background, crowdfunding offers an interesting possibility to finance the start-up in the beginning.

I am also convinced that funding start-ups via the company building of the incubators will increase. Usually successful internet company owner, who had an successful exit, open an incubator to support new founder teams during the idea-shaping. They will also finance the teams in the beginning.

## Dr. Carsten Rudolph

What is your opinion on crowdfunding?

Generally, crowdinvesting sounds like a great opportunity for start-ups, but current models in Germany (I do not know the others) have several, sometimes strong limitations. Current models make follow-on investments very difficult due to legal constructions, so it only works for start-up needing only few money in total. The cost is fairly high with 10-12 % of the money raised, but still the platforms do not earn sufficient money. And last not least, Crowdinvesting draws some people interested in start-ups, the "wide general public" still does not understand the mechanics, and there will be still a long time until that will really happen. So far everyone seems to be happy, but we did not have a failure of a crowd-funded start-up. Wait till then…

But crowdfunding is an interesting model for a very limited number of start-up that have immediately useable consumer goods, where the funder has an immediate benefit being one of the first persons using the new item (prestige, image, interest in innovation).

According to the current numbers, crowdfunding seems to be the future of financing a start up. What is your opinion on that?

Crowdfunding is only appropriate for a limited number of start-ups. The majority will have to look for other sources, in particular in industrial fields, b2b applications etc. So, I do not agree. It will take a certain share, but definitely not the majority.

How could the future of financing a start-up look like?

I think there is a lot of space in private Business Angel financing in the range of 150k€ to 1m €. We have seen this segment growing in the last few years, and this will continue to grow, provided the right intermediaries such as well managed (!) angel networks. Private investors, such as Business Angels, together with public-co-investing will have an increasing role in start-up financing.

## Andreas Unseld

What is your opinion on crowdfunding?

Crowdfunding is currently a big hype and seems to make sense for start-ups, which need not a huge amount of money. Small investments are not interesting for investors, because the costs of the new venture (due diligence, management, etc.) are very high, therefore crowdfunding is a possibility for start-ups, which require less. But I see two main problems: The acceptance by the crowd when the first project will fail and the overall legal situation, which has not been proofed en detail yet.

According to the current numbers, crowdfunding seems to be the future of financing a start up. What is your opinion on that?

It is a question about the amount of money. But also for smaller amounts of money crowdfunding will stay a small area, because the entrepreneurs need "free" money for their start-up. They need it for rent, loans, development, etc. and not only for production. I am not sure, if the donation model will work. It is always a question about the purpose and there is no business model, which is built on donation.

How could the future of financing a start-up look like?

In my opinion the VC trend will decrease and there will be more investments by individuals. These private persons might invest more than 10.000 Euros. Secondly IT-start-ups will be more capital efficient. The average amount of money, which will be needed, might be about 200.000 Euro until break-even. Therefore the typical VC advancement will also decrease.

## 8.4    Other specialists

Prof. Frank Piller

What is your opinion on crowdfunding?

Crowdfunding is not new. There have always been companies who sold things first and then started to produce them. In some companies this is part of the business model.

According to the current numbers, crowdfunding seems to be the future of financing a start up. What is your opinion on that?

I am sure that crowdfunding will be another financing channel in the future for start-ups, but there are some disadvantages. The new enterprises get a huge pressure to really produce the products and send them to people who already paid. But it is not only the pressure to really get into action, but also the team has to tell the idea very early, which is always somehow dangerous. Crowdfunding is good for the time after the prototypes have been produced, but it is not a good solution to finance the very early stage and idea development.

How could the future of financing a start-up look like?

This is difficult to say. There will be always the usual form of financing. Companies will use crowdfunding not only for financing, but also for marketing reasons and word-of-mouth. Where is then the border to interactive marketing? And last but not least: Not every idea fits for crowdfunding.

## René S. Klein, journalist fuer-gruender.de

What is your opinion on crowdfunding?

Crowdfunding as well as crowdinvesting represents a very good alternative and additional way to finance projects as well as start-ups. It can make it easier for start-ups to gain access to financial means. In general I think crowdinvesting is more efficient than crowdfunding for financing a start-up in Germany. But I doubt that we will reach circumstances like Kickstarter in the US.

According to the current numbers, crowdfunding seems to be the future of financing a start up. What is your opinion on thaournalis?

It will be part of the future but not "the future". We will always have the traditional Business Angels and VCs to finance start-ups. We shall not forget that start-ups still need to deliver their promises - also to crowd. And not all start-ups will be successful and the crowd will become more selective.

The public funding period can as well be perceived as an excellent opportunity for the start-up to get some opinion and feedback about its business idea and the product or services. You can also call it market research although it does not equal a profound market study of course. Additionally a marketing effect seems to be obvious with regard to the funding period and every supporter can be a micro marketing manager for the company. But the extend of these effects is difficult to measure and varies from project to project.

How could the future of financing a start-up look like?

Start-ups will be more likely and able to combine the

different ways. That means that the sources of funding become more divers. Crowdfunding enriches the financing opportunities for start-ups but of course will never be a substitute for VCs. Nevertheless VCs might rethink their role and probably try to act different in the future as they get some competition for ideas. They are not alone anymore but most compete with alternative funding sources.